Genre Fairy Tale

 Essential Question
How do we get what we need?

The Chickpea Boy

ᕉᕉ A Persian Fairy Tale ᕉᕉ

retold by **Frederica Brown**
illustrated by **Robert Dunn**

Chapter 1

Out of the Soup

One day, a poor and humble woman was cooking some soup for herself and her husband. As she finished, she wished she had a child of her own. To her great surprise, a chickpea hopped out of the pot and turned into a little boy.

"Who are you?" cried the woman. "Where did you come from?"

"Hello, Mother," said the Chickpea Boy. "I am the child you wished for! Shall I take some soup to Father?"

The woman dished up a bowl of soup, and the Chickpea Boy carried it carefully to the table.

"Hello, Father!" said the Chickpea Boy. "Here is some soup that Mother has made."

"Who are you?" asked the man.

"I am your son," replied the Chickpea Boy.

"You are?" said the man. "Then you can do a job for me. I loaned the king a coin. Go and ask him for it back. You might have to barter. The king sees no need to honor his debt. He considers himself above everyone else."

STOP AND CHECK

Where did the Chickpea Boy come from?

Chapter 2
Off to See the King

The Chickpea Boy set off. He walked until he came to a stream. There was a woman washing clothes. The Chickpea Boy asked her to wash his cap.

"No, I will not wash your cap," said the woman. "I have enough washing to do!"

"You won't be able to do any washing
now!" said the Chickpea Boy. He stooped
down and drank the whole stream dry. Then
he went on again, leaving the woman staring
after him.

A little farther on, a leopard jumped out.

"Where are you going?" asked the leopard.

"I'm going to collect a coin from the king," said the Chickpea Boy.

"Can I come, too?" asked the leopard.

"It's a long way," said the Chickpea Boy.

"You could give me a ride," said the leopard.

"Jump in," said the Chickpea Boy.

He opened his mouth, and the leopard jumped in.

A little farther on, a wolf jumped out. "Where are you going?" asked the wolf.

"I'm going to collect a coin from the king," said the Chickpea Boy.

"Can I come, too?" asked the wolf.

"It's a long way," said the Chickpea Boy.

"You could give me a ride," said the wolf.

"Jump in," said the Chickpea Boy.

He opened his mouth, and the wolf jumped in.

A little farther still, a jackal jumped out. "Where are you going?" asked the jackal.

"I'm going to collect a coin from the king," said the Chickpea Boy.

"Can I come, too?" asked the jackal.

"It's a long way," said the Chickpea Boy.

"You could give me a ride," said the jackal.

"Jump in," said the Chickpea Boy.

He opened his mouth, and the jackal jumped in.

STOP AND CHECK

Why didn't the woman wash the Chickpea Boy's cap?

Chapter 3

At the King's Court

At last the Chickpea Boy arrived at the king's court. Just as the father had said, the king did not want to pay back the coin. The king ordered his servants to throw the Chickpea Boy to his fighting birds.

"He'll be pecked to pieces," said the king.

The servants left the Chickpea Boy alone with the fighting birds. As soon as he was alone, he opened his mouth. The wolf and the jackal jumped out and caught all the birds. Then they both went home. When the king's servants came back in the morning, they found the Chickpea Boy waiting for them.

The servants took the news to the king.

"Throw him in the zoo! The beasts will deal with him," said the king. The servants did as they were told. As soon as the Chickpea Boy was alone, he opened his mouth. Out jumped the leopard, who ate up all the beasts.

When the king's servants came in the morning, they found the Chickpea Boy safe and sound.

The servants took the news to the king.

"Throw him into a room of burning
straw!" ordered the king. "The smoke will
be too much for him."

The servants did as they were told.
But as soon as the Chickpea Boy was alone,
he opened his mouth. The water from the
stream poured out and put out the fire.
Then he went to sleep, and the king's
servants found him still snoozing
next morning.

The king didn't know what to do.
He asked his wisest advisor.

"I don't think we will get the better of
this boy," said the advisor. "Best give him
a coin in payment and tell him to be off."

"I hate to admit it," said the king, "but
I think you are right."

Reluctantly, the king ordered his servants to take the Chickpea Boy to the treasure room. They did as they were told. As soon as he was alone in the magnificent room, the Chickpea Boy opened his mouth. He swallowed as much gold and silver as he could. Then he took one coin in his hand and went home.

When the Chickpea Boy got home, he handed the coin to his father. He hugged his mother. As she patted him on the back, his mouth opened, and the gold and silver came pouring out. They were no longer poor and humble. They were rich.

STOP AND CHECK

Why did the Chickpea Boy take one coin in his hand?

Respond to Reading

Summarize

Use details from the story to summarize *The Chickpea Boy.* Your chart may help you.

Details

↓

Point of View

Text Evidence

1. How can you tell this story is a fairy tale? Identify one feature that tells you this. Genre

2. What can you tell about the Chickpea Boy from his actions?
   Point of View

3. What does the word *carefully* on page 3 mean? Use the root word *care* to help you find out. Root Words

4. Describe the Chickpea Boy from the king's point of view. Write about Reading

Compare Texts
Read how gold has always been treasured.

Forgotten Gold

Imagine finding buried treasure! Some people have been lucky enough to do so.

In 1922, an archeologist found the tomb of Tutankhamun. Tutankhamun, a king of Egypt, lived more than 3,000 years ago. His tomb was filled with beautiful objects. Many of these amazing creations were made of pure gold.

Archeologists have found many gold treasures from the ancient world.

This gold mask was found in Tutankhamun's tomb.

Hisham Ibrahim/Photodisc/Getty Images

Archeologists have found gold jewelry and utensils, or tools. They've found gold weapons, too. But gold is a soft metal, so the weapons were for decoration.

Gold objects, like this cup, were treasured.

Some ancient people used gold to barter, or swap one kind of goods for another. Then people began to make gold coins. Coins were given a value according to how much gold was actually in them.

Uses of Gold in the Ancient World

Egypt statues, jewelry, ornaments, furniture, coins	**Greece** jewelry, coins, ornaments, utensils	**Rome** coins (called *aureus*), jewelry, utensils

Ancient gold coins have been found by people with metal detectors.

Ancient gold coins are found quite often. Some of these gold treasures belonged to people who lived more than 1,000 years ago. Today, some people collect gold coins from the ancient world.

Make Connections

How did ancient people use gold?

Essential Question

What do *The Chickpea Boy* and *Forgotten Gold* tell you about wealth?

Text to Text

Focus on
Genre

Fairy Tales Fairy tales are fantasy stories. They are not realistic and can include magical events. Fairy tales are often retold by different authors.

Read and Find *The Chickpea Boy* is a fairy tale with an amazing central character. The author has retold the story in her own words.

Your Turn

How do you think that the humble man and woman felt when the Chickpea Boy returned with great wealth, not just one coin? Write a sequel to the story. What happened next?